(CONTENT
CONTENIDO
THE ROBERTO MARTINEZ STORY

DESIGNED AND PRODUCED BY

Editor Darren Griffiths • **Chief Writer** Hamish Dufton
Design, Writing and Production James Cleary and Graeme Helliwell
Photography Press Association and Tony Woolliscroft

ARRIVAL - ROBERTO AT FINCH FARM

The manager parks up at Everton's
training HQ prepared for another busy day...

Few would have expected just how resounding an impact Roberto Martinez would have here at Everton Football Club.

When the time came to choose a manager to take the Club forward in a bold new direction, the Spaniard's name was perennially linked to the Goodison Park hot seat. Many, including Chairman Bill Kenwright, had that name at the top of their wish lists.

And unveiled he was, now customary brown shoes and all, as Everton's new manager.

But just who is Roberto Martinez? Where has he come from? What has shaped the footballing ethos that has dazzled opposition and supporters alike?

This special magazine delves into the past of our charismatic manager, charting his early introduction to the beautiful game as a youngster growing up in Balaguer in Spain, through his formative years as a young pro at Real Zaragoza to the unexpected career path that took him to Wigan Athletic as part of the Three Amigos.

Read the thoughts of those who came and went throughout that journey from street football to the FA Cup final via the Football Leagues, including the man who first brought him to England, Dave Whelan, former team-mates Lee Trundle and Dennis Lawrence, and those who played under him.

This is the remarkable story that shaped the character, beliefs and methods of Roberto Martinez, told by the man himself and those who have been privileged enough to work with him.

And the best bit? The Everton chapter of this story has only just begun...

BILL KENWRIGHT:

"I INSTANTLY THOUGHT HE HAD THE PERSONALITY THAT COULD TAKE THIS FOOTBALL CLUB ON..."

Prior to Roberto Martinez, Everton Football Club had only ever employed 13 different full-time managers in its history. So the responsibility of appointing a new man at the end of last term was undeniably an enormous and extremely onerous remit.

"I didn't look upon it like that," smiled Bill Kenwright. "The fans had supported my choice of David Moyes and I never had the feeling that I wouldn't be supported this time around, which was very important to me. I know what Evertonians want and more than anything they want class, style and a football club that they can not only believe in, but one they can admire.

"The main problem was that we truly did not know David was going until towards the end of the season."

But from the moment that David Moyes' departure was formally confirmed, Bill was met with a deluge of applications for the vacancy and a curious football world embarked on endless rounds of speculation and prediction. For the first time in 11 years the Chairman didn't have a manager...but a seed had been planted during the spring.

"Like every single Evertonian on that horrible day in the FA Cup quarter-final I was devastated," he said. "But that afternoon I looked at the opposition manager and thought he was a bit special. And something else was that David had always thought Wigan were a tough nut to crack.

Bill was in attendance to see Roberto lead Wigan Athletic to FA Cup glory (opposite page)

"I actually went to the FA Cup final when Wigan beat Manchester City and I spent 90 minutes looking at the manager more than the game. At first I thought it was going to be really tough but Wigan held firm and then came into the game slowly but surely. When they brought on Ben Watson with nine minutes left I told Jenny, my wife that they were going to win it."

Having watched his own side being dismantled at the last-eight stage of the competition, it wasn't a straightforward decision for Bill to go to Wembley. His day-out at football's HQ almost ended before it had begun!

"It's the only time I've been to a final without Everton. If it's not us I try to forget FA Cup final day! I went at the last moment. I didn't leave my house until 20 minutes before kick-off. When I got there I had left my tickets at home but luckily someone recognised me. The guy in charge of the Bobby Moore Club let us in because he'd played Neil Sedaka's dad, Maxi the Taxi, for me in the Neil Sedaka Story the year before!"

Bill walked away from Wembley that day with the name Roberto Martinez firmly in his mind. The very first meeting between the two confirmed his cup final day thoughts. The Chairman had known 'instantly' that he would appoint David Moyes within moments of their first conversation back in March 2002, and his inaugural meeting with Roberto was exactly the same.

"If I am good at anything, it's judging character," said Bill. "I spoke to a lot of people from within the game and I saw a lot of potential candidates, of which Roberto was one. When he walked into my office I instantly thought he had the personality that could take this football club on.

"He told me that

Everton should be in the Champions League, which I then repeated at his media unveiling to some press amusement. He said that Everton should have a dream and that dream should be Champions League football. You can't buy positivity like that."

Being certain in your own mind that you are about to make the correct call on an incredibly big decision that will ultimately affect so many people must be a wonderful feeling. One of overwhelming relief perhaps?

"Relief is too negative a word," countered Bill. "Safe is a better word for it. That feeling of security when you know your search is over."

Once Roberto had been offered the position of manager of Everton Football Club he brought with him exactly the sort of energy, enthusiasm and vibrancy that Bill had anticipated.

"We drove together to Finch Farm for his first visit and I saw the look on his face when we got there. He was like a kid at Disneyland and he said, 'Chairman, I'm in Blue Heaven!' Then when we introduced him to the press at Goodison a few hours later the atmosphere was one of celebration.

"I love what he's brought to the club, that feeling of real optimism. Roberto has such enthusiasm, style, PR skills, people skills, a real conviction...and most of all real, real talent and commitment.

"The first three drawn games of the season were not easy for him because of the uncertainty surrounding Bainesy and Felli. It's no coincidence that once that was over, we started winning. Roberto handled it brilliantly."

The man from Balaguer made a big impression at Everton from the moment he breezed through the Goodison gates for the very first time, and the Chairman continues to be impressed.

"We had a meeting in my office not long ago and his focus is awesome. I have never come across anyone who knows more about football. He's 24/7 football. He talks to me about how almost every other team in world football plays the game. He told me that he has adjoining sofas at home that meet at an angle so that his wife Beth can watch her TV at one end and he can watch football at the other!

"Everton are blessed to have him and I don't believe that anyone doubts that we have made the right choice."

Few in football will argue with that.

PRIMEROS DIAS

(EARLY DAYS)

From birth, Roberto was a born winner. Inspired
by his father's will-to-win mentality, the youngster
developed a thirst for footballing knowledge.
Growing up in the small Catalan town of Balaguer,
he caught the eye of Real Zaragoza scouts when
playing for his local youth side – and the first steps
on his path towards Goodison had begun

I t was in Balaguer on 13 July 1973 that Roberto and Amor Martinez celebrated the arrival of a baby son. They called the boy Roberto…

The future Everton manager's father, Roberto Martinez senior, was born in Zaragoza and played football for various teams across Spain before signing for Balaguer. It was there that he met the woman who would later become his wife, Amor. Roberto senior had met the love of his life but it meant that his football travelling days were over!

"That's when my mum told him that she wasn't moving anywhere so my dad could only manage in that area!" Roberto junior recalled. "One of my first memories as a child is that every Sunday I would be taken to watch my father play football. My first contact with a football came when I was two years old. My father would take me onto the pitch for a couple of hours before the game and teach me to kick the ball back and forth to him. In primary school I was the envy of all the other boys because my father would give me the professional balls once his team had finished with them! As

> **My first contact with a ball came when I was two. My father would take me onto the pitch and teach me to kick the ball back and forth to him**

I got older I would still watch his teams although by then he was a manager. He managed Balaguer and then other teams around the local area but it was more of a hobby for him really."

Roberto senior and Amor installed many admirable disciplines into their two children, Roberto junior and his sister, Antonieta, and in particular, the young boy inherited his father's strong will to win.

"Whenever there was an opportunity, my father and I would play games against each other. Neither of us wanted to lose and that winning mentality, which I got from him, was a great learning process as well as being excellent preparation for being a professional sportsman. The competition was fierce, even when there was no ball involved. Cards, Ludo or any board game – it didn't matter what we played, the atmosphere would be incredibly intense as we both

pushed for victory!"

From a very young age, football played a large part in young Roberto's life. Just like boys from all over the world, none more so than Merseyside, he honed his skills by kicking a ball about in the streets surrounding the family home.

"Oh yes, always," he confirmed. "We would play for hours and hours after school. My mum and dad had a shoe shop and we would always play football outside in the street. Everybody did that in Spain and we used the way the streets were constructed to improve our skills. We would find little parts of the street or the main square in the town, with maybe an uneven surface to practice technique.

"We had one really long street and along it there were tall columns. We used to see who would be the first one to dribble the ball up and down and hit every column along the way. It was a great way to learn.

Young Roberto was a footballer from a young age...

"There were 15,000 people living in the town and it was a perfectly safe environment for us to grow up in and play our football in the street."

When he compares his own playing style with that of his father, Roberto is honest enough to concede that a determination not to lose was probably the only attribute they had in common!

"My father was always a very aggressive and strong player," he said. "He was more of a defender than anything else. Since my first game as a youngster I was always a midfielder. I sometimes played wide but most of the time I played in the middle of the park. People who have seen us both play would probably agree that our styles were as different as day and night!"

> ## My father and I would play games against each other. Neither of us wanted to lose and that winning mentality was a great learning process as well as being excellent preparation for being a sportsman

Young Roberto soon showed that he was more than capable with a football at his feet but it was always a case of 'schoolwork first, then your football.' His father knew only too well the potential pitfalls of professional football and so he was determined that his son's education wouldn't suffer.

"Yes, he was quite strong on that and so was my mum but I was quite happy with that," said Roberto. "I knew how important that was."

When Roberto was at school in Balaguer he played 'Futbol Sala', which is a five-a-side variation of football and was played in all Spanish schools.

"For as long as I can remember, back to the age of five or six we would play Futbol Sala for the school team all the way through to 16 or 17," he said.

Roberto's home town of Balaguer, in NE Spain

ROBERTO'S...
...BALAGUER

The town is the capital of the comarca (county) of Noguera in Catalonia, Spain.

It is picturesque and historic, but a largely unremarkable town that stands on the River Serge.

A Gothic bridge, the 'Pont de Sant Miquel', crosses the river and the impressive Santa Maria Church watches down over the town.

Roberto's local club, CF Balaguer, played in the Primera Catalana - Group 2 in 2013/14, a regional level equivalent to the fifth tier of Spanish football.

He loaned two young Welsh players to the club when manager of Swansea: Chad Bond and Kerry Morgan.

SPAIN

BALAGUER ●
ZARAGOZA ●
MADRID ●

"From the age of 11, we would also play 11-a-side football, which meant that we would play on Saturday and Sunday. Futbol Sala is the best way of developing technically and tactically for a young player. It's four versus four with a smaller ball that didn't bounce so you had to use your skills. Playing in such an enclosed area means that you can grow as a player and learn a lot technically.

"It's a great way to develop youngsters and allows the player to develop himself, encouraging their raw talent to shine and enjoy the game while polishing skills and increasing fitness levels."

As he played for fun with his friends, young Roberto had an inkling from an early age that, without bragging about it in any way, shape or form, he had more natural football ability

than those who joined in the games. He stood out in the way that the more gifted children do during matches.

"Well, I could see that in my teams I was the one scoring the goals. You could see who was making the difference between winning and losing the games. I experienced my first competitive game for Balaguer's youth team when I was nine years old. The first team played in the fourth tier of the professional game. They had youth teams all the way through to the age of 18 and then you had the B team and the first team, but I left when I was 16."

When Roberto was 16 years old he was invited to play for Real Zaragoza in a youth tournament against teams of the calibre of Real Madrid and Barcelona. The young midfielder scored against Madrid and impressed sufficiently to be offered a contract – news that received a mixed reaction in the Martinez household!

"Zaragoza is a two-hour drive from Balaguer so it was a big move for me because I obviously had to move away from my family," he explained. "My dad was okay because he was born in

Roberto hasn't changed a bit...

Zaragoza but my mum wasn't so pleased. My mum told me that as long as I studied for my degree I would be allowed to go. My dad warned me not to go there and start drinking and smoking and thinking I had made it as a professional footballer. But I assured him that I wouldn't do those things. I promised to concentrate on my studies and my football. That was the agreement."

Roberto's chosen subject to extend his studies beyond school was physiotherapy. He managed to successfully combine his education and his sport, even though it was tough at times, especially as he was living with friends and was far away from the protective attention of his parents!

"I got my degree at the University of Zaragoza at the same time that I was playing. I always wanted to know my body and I wanted to study something that would be related to sport. I wasn't into fitness or coaching at that time, I wanted a proper degree with a medical background. At the time physiotherapy was a fairly new degree in Spain and you had to have good A-Levels to get

onto the course. The first year was very intense with all the theory, but the second and third years were more practical and it was a great experience for me.

"It was great because it was a real challenge to carry on with my studies. In Spain, once boys got to 18 they tended to just concentrate on football and not studying but it was important for me to carry on and get my degree in physiotherapy because it helped me to know my body.

"I hardly had a bad injury in my career. I knew how to prepare myself and I knew how to work on injury prevention. The worst injury I had during my playing career was a ruptured medial knee ligament at Swansea and that was an accident during a game.

"It was hard linking the intensive study with the demanding training schedules at the football club. I used the two different experiences to give me a balance in my life. When I had a bad time on the training ground or in a match I would concentrate on my course and enjoy the stimulus of academic work. In the same way, if I had a bad time in the examination room I would look forward to getting rid of all my tension and anxiety on the football pitch.

"The university was extremely helpful as they knew I was playing for Real Zaragoza. They would often

Real Zaragoza's La Romareda stadium

Zaragoza is a two-hour drive from Balaguer so it was a big move for me because I had to move away from my family...my dad warned me not to go there and start drinking and smoking, thinking I had made it

change the times of examinations to fit in with matches or training."

Always high on the list of considerations for a young boy leaving home for the first time to pursue a career is living accommodation. Real Zaragoza were very wise with their choice of home for their young footballers and Roberto forged a friendship with his first landlady that continues to endure today.

"I was in club digs when I first went to Zaragoza," he said. "I stayed with a really nice family that I had great feelings for. Even now, every time I get the chance to go back to Zaragoza I go and see Gloria.

"We had 10 bedrooms and we would all eat together. Gloria would cook for all of us and some of the first-team players would come as well to eat the food!"

Roberto made his Real Zaragoza debut when he was 19 years of age. It was the final match of the 1992/93 season and the first team were away at Atletico Madrid. A certain Gustavo Poyet was injured and unable to take part so coach Victor Fernandez handed Roberto a place on the bench. He came off it in the second half to replace Luis Carlos Cuartero. Nayim, the former Tottenham Hotspur player, was alongside him in the Zaragoza line-up.

"I remember it being a great atmosphere. The charismatic Jesus Gil was their president at the time. It was the final game of the season and we were leading at one point but it ended 2-2. It was a great experience for me. Atletico needed Real Madrid to win La Liga so they themselves could guarantee

qualification for Europe but such is the rivalry that their supporters wanted Real to lose so they wouldn't win the league, even though that meant Atletico wouldn't qualify for Europe! In our game the Atletico fans were cheering when they found out that Real Madrid were losing against Tenerife. It was a significant day."

Tenerife defeated Madrid 2-0 to hand the La Liga title to Barcelona and the following week saw Real Zaragoza competing in the final of the Spanish Cup, the Copa del Rey. Poyet was back and Roberto didn't make the bench but he still enjoyed the experience, despite the fact that Zaragoza lost 2-0 to Real Madrid in Valencia.

"Just to be around the dressing room was a huge experience for me," he said. "I was really young and it was all new and exciting.

"The football philosophy at Zaragoza was great to get involved with. Zaragoza was a team that could beat anyone on their day, even Real Madrid and Barcelona. But we couldn't compete against them in a league campaign and that's why Zaragoza became such a good cup team."

They proved that the following season when they again reached the final of the Copa del Rey and this time they won it, defeating Celta Vigo on penalties at the Vincente Calderon Stadium in Madrid. That win put them into the 1994/95 European Cup Winners' Cup competition, which they won, defeating Arsenal in the final in Paris.

"Zaragoza is a club with a great

Nayim's 120th-minute strike from near the touchline clinches the 1995 European Cup Winners' Cup for Roberto's Real Zaragoza

> ▌ **Zaragoza is a club with a great tradition with a great taste for good football and it was a good place for me to start looking into the games and wanting to win them with style. I saw the style and I liked it.**

Roberto's football and university education was developed in Zaragoza

tradition with a great taste for good football. It was a good place for me to start looking into the games and wanting to win them with style," said Roberto. "I saw the style and I liked it. I had no choice really because I grew up in that style and it's something I've kept since then."

At the end of the 1994/95 campaign, when Nayim's long-range effort from close to the touchline deceived David Seaman to clinch that European trophy for Real Zaragoza, Roberto received his call-up papers for National Service.

"It was at the back end of the national service and the length of service had gone down from two years to nine months," he recalled. "Previously you had to do national service, you had no choice, but when I became eligible people had a choice and I was able to work for the Balaguer council teaching football to young children. I played for the Balaguer first team while I did this.

"That's when I started coaching at the age of 20. As well as coaching the young players and organising the matches I was also in charge of co-ordinating the work of the individual coaches who looked after the different age groups."

Roberto never really managed to establish himself at Real Zaragoza and at the end of the 1994/95 season he was ready to leave the La Romareda stadium for a change in direction. However, not even he could have dreamt just how dramatic the alteration to his football path would be!

ROBERTO'S...
...REAL ZARAGOZA

Real were founded in 1932, formed from two rival teams: Iberia SC and Real Zaragoza CD.

Nicknamed 'Los Blanquillos' (The Whites), the side currently play in the Segunda Division, having been relegated in 2013.

Real have never won La Liga, finishing as runners-up in 1974/75 – but have won six Copa del Reys, the last one in 2004.

As well as securing European Cup Winners' Cup glory in 1994/95, Zaragoza have also been victorious in European competition in the Inter-Cities Fairs Cup – the forerunner of the UEFA Cup and Europa League – in 1963/64.

Everton (pictured setting off for Spain) have previously met Real Zaragoza in competitive action, over two legs in the second round of the European Cup Winners' Cup in 1966/67. In November 1966 the Blues went down 2-0 in Spain in the first leg, before defeating Real 1-0 at Goodison thanks to a Sandy Brown goal, thereby bowing out 2-1 on aggregate. Zaragoza lost in the following round to Rangers on the toss of a coin after the quarter-final tie had ended level.

Cafu, Andreas Brehme, Jose Luis Chilavert, Frank Rijkaard, Pablo Aimar, David Villa and Ruben Sosa have all played for Zaragoza. Ex-players with links to English football include Helder Postiga, Savo Milosevic, Fernando Morientes, Nayim, Gerard Pique and Gustavo Poyet.

WHAT'S ON
THE AGENDA?

Roberto goes through the day's events
with his secretary, Sue Palmer

BIENVENIDO A INGLATERRA

(WELCOME TO ENGLAND)

The persuasive Dave Whelan brought Roberto and fellow Spaniards, Jesus Seba and Isidro Diaz, to English football – the first to play in the Football League for over 40 years

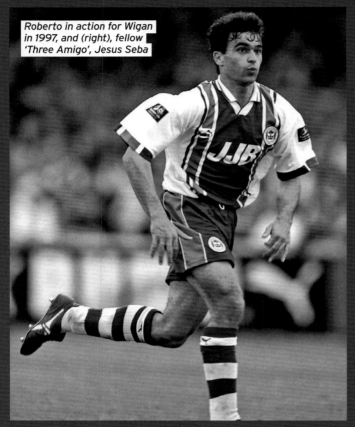

Roberto in action for Wigan in 1997, and (right), fellow 'Three Amigo', Jesus Seba

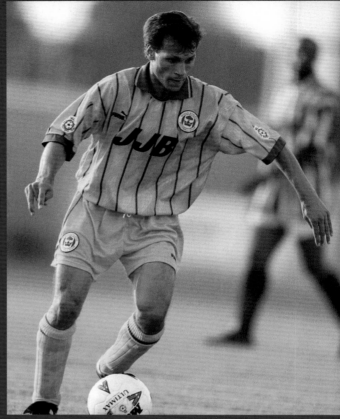

Zaragoza in Spain is 826 miles from the Lancashire town of Wigan but for Roberto Martinez, it was a whole new world when he swapped La Liga for the third tier of English football. A more unlikely transfer you would struggle to imagine – but then the new owner of Wigan Athletic Football club wasn't big on orthodox routes. He was, however, a very perceptive and persuasive individual…

"Dave Whelan opened JJB Sport shops in Spain," Roberto began. "He opened four in Zaragoza, Majorca, Barcelona and Bilbao and the manager of those shops was an ex-footballer. Dave told this guy that he had just bought a football club in England and he wanted to bring some flair into the squad. He wanted something different, technically. The manager of the shops was based in Zaragoza and so that's how the opportunity came around for me. He saw us play at Zaragoza and offered us the opportunity."

So that was phase one of the operation completed. All Dave Whelan had to do now was persuade Roberto Martinez,

Jesus Seba and Isidro Diaz to swap life on the River Ebro for life on the Manchester Ship Canal. Once again, Roberto was to discover that what Dave Whelan wants, Dave Whelan normally gets.

"Dave asked us to come over to Wigan for a week in July 1995, have a look around and give him the opportunity to tell us what he wanted to do," said Roberto. "We were accompanied by our agent and we always had someone with us from JJB Sports who could speak Spanish. Everyone who dealt with us that week made us feel special and welcome. They even organised a trip to Blackpool and, somehow, it was on a sunny day. We even told our friends and families that it was not very different from Spain.

"Dave went out of his way to make us feel that he wanted us to sign for the club. From that point on we were engaged with him and the project he was putting together. Wigan was in the fourth tier then but Dave had a project and a vision and he told us that within 10 years he wanted the team to be in the Premier League playing at a new stadium. Everything he told us became a reality.

Wigan owner Dave Whelan (above) played for Blackburn in the 1960 FA Cup final

"He was very persuasive and that's one of the biggest qualities that Dave Whelan has. When he has a vision or a dream he just does everything right to achieve it. Everything he touches becomes gold and that's a lot down to his persistence and the way he can engage with others. We were blown away by his plan and we wanted to be part of it."

It was a new, exciting and completely different challenge for Roberto and he acknowledges to this day that the fact that three Spaniards made the incredible journey helped.

"Jesus Seba had played for Spain Under-21s, Isidro Diaz was in the first-team squad with me and we were young, promising boys who were given this wonderful opportunity. It was different and we discussed it between ourselves and agreed to come together. Looking back, if only one of us had come over it would never have lasted. It would have been impossible. At that time there were no other Spanish players playing in the Football League and there was a completely different perception of what Spanish players could bring to the English game."

The project that some had thought unlikely at best was beginning to

(Below) Isidro Diaz, who enjoyed two spells at Wigan from 1995-1998

> If only one of us had come over it would never have lasted. There were no Spanish players in the League and there was a completely different perception of what Spanish players could bring to English football

ROBERTO'S...

...SPANISH FOOTBALLERS IN ENGLISH FOOTBALL

Prior to the signing of 'The Three Amigos' in the summer of 1995, only three Spanish players had played in the Football League.

Emilio Aldecoa was the first, playing a season at Coventry City after the Second World War. Born in Bilbao in 1922, the winger also played War-time football for Wolves, having arrived in England in 1937 as a refugee from the Spanish Civil War. He was later capped by his country and won two league titles with Barcelona.

Jose and Antonio Gallego were also refugees from the Spanish Civil War. Jose was the more successful, a forward who played at Brentford, Colchester United and Southampton in the late 1940s and early-1950s. Antonio's career was briefer, turning out once as a goalkeeper for Norwich City in 1947.

One other notable 'Spanish' influence which was curbed before it really began came in November 1954. A former Barcelona midfielder, Hungarian-born Elemer Berkessy became the Football League's first foreign manager with Grimsby Town – having previously coached Roberto's first professional club, Real Zaragoza. His stint was a short one, however, with the authorities denying him an extension to his initial work permit. So just a few months after England had been thrashed 7-1 by Hungary's 'Mighty Magyars' and a year since their 6-3 humbling at Wembley, the attitude appeared to be: 'What could the English learn from one of their countrymen?'

And the first Spanish international to play in the Premier League? Barcelona full-back ALBERT FERRER, who joined Chelsea in the summer of 1998.

DAVE WHELAN: "ROBERTO AS A CHARACTER IS No. 1..."

No Roberto Martinez story would be complete without a contribution from the man who enticed him to England all those years ago.

Dave Whelan has been a pivotal component of this remarkable football tale, and he spoke exclusively about his relationship with the current Everton manager and where it all began...

"I opened some shops in Spain and one of my managers used to watch football matches over there," he began. "He rang me one day to say that he'd seen a Spanish Third Division game and that there were three players who I might be interested in for my football club. So I went over to have a look myself and I liked what I saw. My man was quite right, they were good footballers, three pure footballers. They got the ball, they kept it and they passed

"Jesus Seba pronounced his name 'hay-zeus' but the Wigan crowd called him Jesus. We played Torquay away one day and we had about 300 of our crowd and they brought out this big banner that said 'JESUS IS A WIGANER' and we've never forgotten that!"

Not only did the Wigan chairman want to change the style of play at Springfield Park, he wanted to instil a new mind-set that he knew was necessary to carry the club forward. After all, when he bought the Latics he had promised Premier League football within 10 years.

"There was a bit of a drinking culture at the time but these three lads were tee-total," he explained. "They were great boys and they set some great examples. No alcohol and bed early before games, that was them. They set the rules and

Cup goal, when he netted against non-League Runcorn in 1995!

The FA Cup success merely confirmed what most people in football knew – Roberto Martinez was destined for bigger things. And that is no slight whatsoever on Wigan Athletic Football Club because Dave Whelan is in complete agreement.

"When we lost Roberto I knew it was going to happen," he said. "I've always said to managers, 'If you want to go somewhere I will never stop you' because I think that's wrong. If a manager wants to go to a club that's bigger then it's wrong to stop him going. Football is all about ambition."

And so Dave Whelan waved a reluctant goodbye to Roberto, but the affection that the older man feels for his younger friend is genuine and life-lasting.

"Roberto as a character is number one," said Mr Whelan emphatically. "You will never meet a nicer person than Roberto. His word is his bond. If he says he is going to do something, he does it. I would trust Roberto with my life, he is that kind of man.

"When it comes to football he can be ruthless because you have to be. He knows the game absolutely inside out. He used to play players in certain positions and I would think, 'Roberto, that will never work' but it did!

"He'll go anywhere for his football club. He'll go to schools, he'll go to hospitals to wish people well because he is such a kind man.

"He's never had to ask anyone for their respect because he just has this aura about him that commands respect. I am totally and utterly proud of him and I regard him as one of my great friends in life."

> You will never meet a nicer person. His word is his bond. If he says he is going to do something, he does it. I'd trust Roberto with my life, he's that kind of man

it around, just like Roberto does at Everton now.

"So I spoke to these lads and persuaded them to come over. It wasn't too hard. I told them that the Fourth Division in England was a better and tougher league than they were playing in in Spain. But they were quite keen to come. We signed them on because I wanted to change the style of play at Wigan Athletic when I bought the club.

"It was kick and rush then and I wanted the team to play football. We'd not long come out of the Lancashire Combination, don't forget, and in that league it was 'kick it high and run after it' – but Roberto helped us to change that. As a player he never had a killer instinct in midfield but he would get on the ball and use it brilliantly. These three lads did really well and changed the whole outlook of Wigan Athletic. They were three great boys."

Crucially for Dave Whelan, the supporters at Springfield Park took to the so-called 'Three Amigos' straight away.

regulations, our boys followed and it's done this club the power of good over the years."

When Mr Whelan brought the three Spanish boys over and got to know them really well, he confessed that in the early days he didn't think he'd one day offer one of them the opportunity to manage his team in English football's top flight!

"No, I didn't," he smiled. "I thought they'd be friends for life though and all three of them are. Roberto actually rang me before he went to Swansea as manager and I wished him good luck, which I always do, and I watched him, I kept an eye on him. I watched my current manager, Uwe Rosler, when he was at Brentford. I do it all the time because a lot of good managers and players come from the lower leagues."

Roberto eventually came back to Wigan as manager and he delivered the FA Cup following an unforgettable 1-0 victory over Manchester City at Wembley in 2013 – a far cry from when he became the first Spaniard to ever score an FA

(Right) Dave Whelan with Sir Alex Ferguson, who's Manchester United treble winners opened Wigan's new stadium in August 1999

come together. A vital component though in the longevity of the so-called 'Three Amigos' were the good people of Wigan. The team had traditionally played second fiddle to the rugby league set-up and the few supporters who did frequent Springfield Park were more accustomed to no-nonsense Scousers like Alex Cribley and Tony Kelly, rather than fleet-footed Spanish playmakers like Roberto Martinez and Jesus Seba!

But if they were approaching their new venture with some trepidation, the Three Amigos needn't have worried. They were greeted with open arms.

"The three of us together were made so welcome at Wigan," recalled Roberto. "The supporters were great, Dave Whelan made us feel at home and a combination of things allowed us to have time to settle in.

"It was an incredible experience, the way everyone helped us in that dressing room. We had many good footballers and good characters. Graeme Jones was in the dressing room, John Doolan, a big Evertonian who'd played for Everton reserves was a young player there, Tony Kelly was a great character. Then there was Chris Lightfoot, Mark Leonard – who began his senior career at Everton – and Neill Rimmer was the captain."

Roberto made an instant impact and the Wigan Athletic fans took to him from the moment he stepped out for his debut. He also made a little bit of history on 11 November 1995 when he became the very first Spanish footballer to score a goal in the FA Cup, netting Wigan's goal in a 1-1 first-round draw against Runcorn at Canal Street.

"That's something that you don't realise at the time," he said. "Now with the amount of Spanish players that we have in the competition it takes on a bit more significance. I think it's one of those stories that you keep for your grandchildren!"

That Roberto started so well in English football is testament not only to his ability with a ball, but also to his strength of character. From operating at Atletico Madrid, Barcelona, Real Socidead and Real Madrid, he was now holding his own at fellow Third Division sides Scunthorpe United, Hartlepool United, Scarborough and

Chris Lightfoot was an early team-mate of Roberto's

Doncaster Rovers.

"The view throughout Britain among football fans was that the Spanish players would be fine in the summer but that they would probably go hiding when the rain and the British winter arrived!

"I was a totally different player from what you tended to have in the old Division Three. I wasn't a good tackler and I wasn't good in the air but I was a good technical player. Winning 50-50 challenges in midfield wasn't my game so you can imagine how much of a culture shock it was!

"I had to develop a real tactical awareness straight away just to be effective for my team-mates. I fitted in really well and it was good for me to be able to score a few goals in my first season as well. I was also selected in the PFA Team of the Year twice in consecutive years."

It's probably fair to surmise that when Dave Whelan claimed his ultimate ambition was to see Wigan Athletic play Premier League football, few, if any, believed him. After all, Roberto joined a club that was just about keeping its head above water in English football's basement division.

It wasn't all plain sailing, though, and a demoralising 6-2 home defeat against Mansfield Town in October 1995 had resulted in Graham Barrow's dismissal. Frank Lord took over as caretaker-manager and it was he who played the Three Amigos in the team for the very first time. Eventually, former Norwich City striker, John Deehan, was appointed as the new manager and he led Wigan to the brink of the play-offs – a last day home defeat to Northampton Town cost the Latics dearly.

But Dave Whelan wasn't one for empty promises and the 1996/97 campaign saw Roberto and Wigan begin their incredible journey...

Having started his Wigan career so well, Roberto was desperately keen to help the club move forwards. The promised land of the Premier League still seemed an impossible dream but every marathon begins with one step – and the 1996/97 campaign was the start for Wigan.

Roberto had been the club's official Player of the Year for 1996 and off the field, too, he was starting to feel very much at home.

"I loved it because the Wigan people were so friendly. We would get people knocking on the door and coming in for coffee! We learned a lot of English by practising with people. Everyone was really nice. It gave me the opportunity to understand what foreign players go through when they come over to the English game. But it would not have been possible had there not been three of us.

"Don't forget that we couldn't speak the language when we first came over. I started to study English at university but it didn't sound anything like what was being spoken in Wigan! But slowly I started to understand everyone but it was a funny period getting there!"

One thing that was in rather short supply in Wigan in the mid-1990s was decent Spanish food. The Three Amigos would have their Spanish-style siesta after training and then scour Wigan looking for Tapas bars, often to no avail. They persevered, though, and eventually found a 'second home' in the town.

"We found an Italian restaurant called Milano's that was run by a Spanish person called Ramon," explained Roberto. "He looked after us extremely well and allowed us to go there for lunch and dinner. He even fitted in with us around our training and siesta times!"

The three could also listen to their favourite Spanish radio station, with the help of satellite. "With the help of Jesus and Isidro, with Ramon creating a little bit of Spain in Wigan, and with the friendship and support of everyone in the town, I was able to acclimatise and I thoroughly enjoyed everything I did."

All the pieces in this ambitious jigsaw fitted together in 1996/97. Wigan won the Third Division title on goals scored over second-placed (and big-spending)

Fulham. The Latics won more games than any other team in the division and they scored more goals, thanks in no small part to a club record 31 from centre-forward Graeme Jones.

"It was terrific because we were buying into Dave Whelan's project by being able to adapt to the British game and winning the league," said Roberto. "Wigan was playing a different way because they had the Spanish players and a different influence. It was great for the whole town because at that time Fulham were spending big to try and get into the Premier League so it was great for us to win the title.

"The playing surface at Springfield Park was first class and the fans really got behind us. The groundsman won the 'Groundsman of the Year' award and that was important because a good pitch helped us in the way we wanted to play."

At the end of that title-winning campaign, the Three Amigos were at the crossroads because they were at the end of their initial two-year contracts. Jesus Seba hadn't figured as much as the other two and so he headed back to Spain but Roberto, despite receiving a number of offers including one from La Liga, and Isidro Diaz decided to stay on at Springfield Park.

"I felt very attached to the club and therefore I wanted to be loyal to them. That is why I signed a four-year contract," said Roberto.

The following few seasons provided Wigan with the opportunity to stabilise themselves in English football's third tier and they picked up a trophy along the way – beating a Millwall team that

Skipper Charlie Bishop and boss John Deehan lift the championship trophy in 1997

Roberto holds off the challenge of Ian Wright, then of Burnley, in February 2000

ROBERTO'S...

...WIGAN ATHLETIC

Founded in 1932, the Latics resided in local leagues before becoming founder members of the Northern Premier League in 1968. Ten years later – and after 34 failed attempts – they were finally elected to the Football League.

Having never reached higher than the third tier of English football, by the mid-1990s average crowds had dropped to below 2,000.

Dave Whelan took over in February 1995 with one his first acts to recruit the 'Three Amigos' – Roberto Martinez, Isidro Diaz and Jesus Seba.

Everton assistant-boss Graeme Jones fired Wigan to promotion from the fourth tier in 1996/97 with 31 league goals.

Football League Trophy winners in 1999, after several near misses the Latics eventually reached the Championship for the first time, in 2003.

The Latics left Springfield Park for the 25,138 capacity DW Stadium, which they currently share with Wigan Warriors rugby league club.

Blues FA Cup winner Matt Jackson was in the side that clinched promotion to the Premier League for the first time, after victory over Reading in May 2005.

The 2005/06 campaign saw Wigan reach the League Cup final and finish 10th in their debut top-flight season.

David Unsworth scored the winning penalty that kept the Latics in the Premier League in 2007, at the expense of Sheffield United.

LEIGHTON BAINES joined Everton months later.

The Roberto Martinez managerial era began in summer 2009...

As well as the current Wigan old-boys at Goodison, others to have played for both sides include 1986/87 title winner Kevin Langley, Stuart Barlow, Marcus Bent and Kevin Kilbane.

included Tim Cahill in the final of the Football League Trophy in 1999, although Roberto missed the final at Wembley through injury.

"I had played in earlier rounds so I still felt part of it and it was a big moment just to be at Wembley. It was also a big moment for the Wigan fans and I really enjoyed it. It was another step for Wigan and you must remember that every step forward was one into the unknown for the football club.

"It was an incredible experience and it helped me massively to see how a football club continues to develop as it moves into unknown territory. It was quite unusual and you don't get that in football. Things that teams achieve have generally been done before but for Wigan it was brand new."

It had been a unique experience for Roberto but in the summer of 2001 circumstances beyond his control precipitated his departure from Wigan Athletic.

"At the end of the 2000/01 season Steve Bruce, the new manager who had taken over from Bruce Rioch, spoke to all the players whose contracts were up. After that meeting I genuinely thought that I would receive a new contract. Unfortunately he was only at the JJB Stadium for a couple of months before he left the club to join Crystal Palace. This left me in a state of limbo without a contract. I had to move on."

Roberto received offers from other League One clubs but such was his loyalty to Wigan that he couldn't countenance the prospect of playing against them so he adopted his 'have boots will travel' attitude and, having worked so hard to adapt to life in England…he headed to Scotland!

DAVID LOWE: "HE WAS REALLY DEDICATED AND JUST WANTED TO GET BETTER AND IMPROVE..."

As an Evertonian, former Wigan forward David Lowe was exceptionally pleased to see his old Latics team-mate Roberto Martinez take the reins at Goodison Park.

The current head of youth at Blackburn Rovers was signed by then Wigan manager, John Deehan, a year after Roberto had moved to Lancashire from Spain. For Lowe, the memories of meeting Roberto for the first time are still vivid.

"When I came back to Wigan he had already arrived with his two Spanish colleagues – the Three Amigos as they were called," he recollects. "John Deehan had brought me back to the club for what was my last spell there as a player.

"Straight away, after training Roberto would want to sit and talk about football, training methods and things like that. Even then you had an idea that he would eventually end up becoming a manager. When he trained, he worked to his maximum. He would go off and do things on his own afterwards or play head tennis with one of the other lads. He was really dedicated from a players' point of view and just wanted to get better and improve as much as he could.

"He mixed really well with the rest of the group. He got involved with everyone and the most alarming thing for me was, even though he was quite young at the time, was that his knowledge of the game was extraordinary.

"He was always talking about different aspects of football and wanted to get as much information as he could. He never had a problem mixing in with the culture of the club and the dressing room."

That contributed to the Spaniard enjoying great success at Wigan – winning the Division Three title and the Football League Trophy.

Lowe is unsurprised that his former team-mate enjoyed such success. "On the pitch he was a

> ## Roberto would want to sit and talk about football, training methods...Even then you had an idea that he would eventually end up becoming a manager

really good footballer in central midfield," he continued. "We used to play a 4-4-2 system and he would be in the middle trying to control the game. He had really good footballing intelligence and game understanding. He had real quality to his technique and his passing. Overall he was a pleasure to play with on and off the pitch.

"You get some guys who come over here to this country and struggle from the word go. But I think Roberto enjoyed the challenge. Certainly that was the impression I got from playing with him at Wigan.

"Since then, he has gone from strength to strength in his football career, then taken the step into management. He has taken Everton on to another level, with a different style of play to his predecessor. It's no surprise to me how successful he has been."

That certainly applies to Martinez's managerial career, the pinnacle of which, thus far, is leading unfancied Wigan to their FA Cup triumph at Wembley in May 2013.

"I was part of the team that helped win the Football League Trophy and the Division Three title many years ago but it was just brilliant to see Roberto take the club to Wembley and win the FA Cup," added Lowe.

"For a team like Wigan to win that competition was unimaginable really but he did a fantastic job. He was, of course, unlucky to be relegated for one reason or another, but it's fair to say he did a magnificent job at Wigan."

Martinez, of course, is ably supported by assistant-manager Graeme Jones, another former Latics team-mate of Lowe. It became apparent early on that the duo had clicked. "They were very friendly with each other," he recounted. "As a player, coming into a dressing room you click with some of the lads more than others. Those two developed a really strong friendship even then, both on the pitch and off it.

"I played alongside Graeme as a second striker when he scored over 30 goals in one season. He was an old type of centre-forward – very tough, very good at link play but who could also find a goal when he needed to. I really enjoyed playing with him as well.

"He is a bit similar to Roberto in that he had that thirst for knowledge, sitting around talking about football, coaching – Graeme was no different. It's no surprise to me that he too has had success in his coaching career as well."

It's that success that Lowe sees Everton reaping the benefits of, with the start to their tenure only serving to support those convictions. "Being an Everton supporter, I hope they can take the club to the limit! I wouldn't like to put any benchmark on them at all really. I think they have started exceedingly well and hopefully they can go from strength to strength, not only this season but obviously in seasons to come.

"Roberto has adopted a different style to David Moyes and generally speaking his rein has begun really well."

David Lowe played over 300 games for Wigan

MEDIA DUTIES –
LIGHTS, CAMERA...

Having fulfilled his requirements for radio
and local media, Roberto prepares himself
for a final TV interview

ASUMIENDO NUEVOS RETOS

(TAKING ON NEW CHALLENGES)

The opportunity to experience another football culture
proved a strong lure when Roberto agreed to join
Motherwell – and he experienced another kind of success
off the pitch – before returning south via the M6

As Roberto Martinez would later discover, his departure from Wigan Athletic was merely a temporary leave of absence. It was a bit of time apart rather than a final divorce!

However, his playing days at the JJB were over at the end of the 2000/01 season and it was to Motherwell that he moved, largely due to the prospect of working with Billy Davies. The current Nottingham Forest boss was the manager at Fir Park when Roberto walked through the door for the first time, ready to take on his latest football challenge.

"I had a few options to stay in England but I felt at that time that nothing would have been as exciting or as motivating as going somewhere new. Scotland,

for one reason or another, appealed to me because it was a different league and a chance to play against teams like Rangers and Celtic," said Roberto. "Also, staying in England wouldn't have given me the same learning curve. It was great to go elsewhere and experiment with something else. I actually had options to go back to Spain but that didn't feel right, either.

"I was also pleased at the thought of working with Billy Davies. He was a very enthusiastic person who was determined to make the club the third force in Scotland behind Rangers and Celtic."

The previous season hadn't been particularly good for Motherwell. They finished in the bottom half of the Scottish Premier League and they

*Roberto in pre-season action
for Motherwell against
Norwich City in 2001*

31

Billy Davies
brought Roberto
north of the
border in 2001

didn't progress very far in either of the domestic cup competitions. So in the summer of 2001, Davies made seven new signings including, of course, Roberto.

"There was a buzz around the club that we could build on the promise of Billy's work. He was a really impressive man and when you meet him you know he is a manager who is going to be able to get you at your best."

Unfortunately, the relationship never got the opportunity to flourish. Motherwell started 2001/02 poorly, losing three and drawing three of their opening six games. After a 3-0 defeat at Ibrox against Rangers in September, Davies was sacked and replaced with Eric Black.

"That was the biggest disappointment for me, that after six weeks Billy got the sack. From that point it was a bit of a wasted move for me," Roberto claimed. "There was no time for Billy to work with a new project and give direction to partnerships on the pitch. I was surprised he wasn't given longer to try and turn things around."

The season turned into a struggle to

ROBERTO'S...
...MOTHERWELL

Formed in 1886, the North Lanarkshire club have been ever-presents in the Scottish top flight since 1984.

Scottish champions once, in 1932, they are also twice Scottish Cup winners (1952, 1991) and Scottish League Cup winners, in 1951.

James McFadden joined Everton from Well in September 2003 – while others who have gone the other way include Tony Thomas and John Spencer.

Former Blues midfielder STUART MCCALL took over as boss in late 2010, leading Well to the Champions League qualifiers for the first time, in 2012, before winning SPL Manager of the Year by guiding them to second place the following campaign.

avoid relegation and it ended up being a two-team fight to avoid the drop. Motherwell survived and St Johnstone went down. Ironically, the Saints centre-forward was none other than Graeme Jones.

"Because of my friendship with Graeme I was sad that Saints got relegated to the First Division," said Roberto.

Two games before the end of one of the most forgettable seasons of Roberto's career, Motherwell Football Club was placed into administration and the termination of his Scottish adventure loomed ever closer.

"I learned a lot because the club got itself into a situation where we were fighting to avoid relegation," said Roberto. "The club went into administration and there was no real support from the SFA or the SPFA. It was a very, very steep learning curve for many non-football reasons.

"The football itself was fine and we had some great games against the Old Firm. We had a lot of good young players coming through and it was a very good league."

One of those young players making strides at Fir Park was a teenager called James McFadden, who would later play 147 games for Everton over two spells.

over Fir Park and although Roberto made some good friends during a challenging period north of the border, he knew that it wouldn't be long before he was on the move again.

"I'd signed a three-year contract but after 10 months the contract was broken and then it was a strange situation. Twenty-two contracts got cancelled. Everything felt wrong but from a football perspective it was a good experience for the wrong reasons. It toughened me up."

There is, however, a charming post-script to Roberto's stay at Motherwell. When he first arrived in Scotland, he stayed at the Moorings Hotel and it was there that he met the woman who would eventually become his wife!

"Beth was studying at Strathclyde University and her time at the hotel was part of her marketing and tourism degree. We have been together ever since and she is a fantastic support and a special person, putting up with the many hours when I am away on football duties."

So when Roberto describes Motherwell as something of 'a wasted move' he is not entirely correct. Or at least, we hope he's not!

From North Lanarkshire, his next port of call was the West Midlands…

> **It was a steep learning curve for many non-football reasons. The football was fine and we had some great games against the Old Firm. We had good young players coming through and it was a very good league**

"Faddy stood out straight away," smiled Roberto. "I always remember we went to France in pre-season and Faddy was a bit of a leader among the young players. He wasn't loud or a naughty boy but he had a few followers around him. He was a left-back then. We watched him play a few games in that position and we all thought that it didn't look right. I played with him in a reserve game at Fir Park and he was left-back. He got the ball and went past two or three players, got into the final third of the field, went past two more and scored a goal. I thought, 'You are never, ever a left-back!'

"From that point he broke into the first team as either a 'number 10' or playing out wide, and he was a phenomenal talent. You could see he had something special."

The storm clouds continued to hover

Future Evertonian James McFadden made a big impression on Roberto

EVERTON STADIUM TOURS
THE GOODISON EXPERIENCE

Book today and enjoy 120 years of history.
Plus all visitors will receive a voucher
to spend in Everton One.*

Adults - £10
Juniors^ - £5

0151 530 5212
stadiumtour@evertonfc.com

*Adults will receive a voucher worth £2 and Juniors £1. ^ A Junior is defined as a person aged 15 years

As the 2001/02 season was progressing it became apparent that Walsall, promoted to the second tier for the first time in their history, were heading towards relegation from the First Division.

In January 2002, in an attempt to stop the slide, Ray Graydon was sacked and Colin Lee installed. Lee did well and steered a troubled ship to safety but he knew he had a rebuilding job to do. Among the new players he recruited in the summer was Roberto Martinez.

"Walsall came along and First Division football was something that I wanted to experience," said Roberto. "Colin Lee was a good guy and it was a good opportunity for me, even though the Motherwell experience had shaken me a bit and left me feeling a bit uneasy about the game itself."

His team-mates at the Bescot Stadium included former Everton midfielder, Vinny Samways, and Jamaican international, Fitzroy Simpson.

"The dressing room at Walsall was very interesting. We had players from Brazil, New Zealand, England, Portugal and Spain. We had a real combination and that's why Walsall did so well to stay in the First Division. That gave me an insight into how to use different strengths and different talents from different cultures, while making sure that you have a good core that sets the direction for the British game.

"It was a fascinating period for me and looking back, I think it prepared me to understand a dressing room and to know how a dressing room full of foreign talent can be very effective."

Such thoughts may have been permeating in his mind but at this stage, Roberto still hadn't considered that his future in the game may be on the coaching side.

"No, I hadn't even thought about it. I was the one telling everyone to keep playing as long as they can and that you should never stop playing until you can't run anymore."

Walsall Football Club is not ideally located when it comes to attracting visitors through the turnstiles. Wolverhampton Wanderers, Aston Villa, Birmingham City, West Bromwich Albion and –until recently – Coventry City are all

Paul Merson (centre) and former Everton midfielder Vinny Samways (right) were team-mates of Roberto

ROBERTO'S...
...WALSALL

Founded in 1888 – the same year as the formation of the Football League – the Saddlers have never played in the top flight, last appearing at Championship level in 2003/04.

They moved to the Bescot Stadium in 1990 – at the time only the second new Football League ground since the 1950s.

Everton have twice met Walsall in domestic cup competition – both at Goodison. In the first season of the League Cup, 1960/61, the Blues prevailed 3-1 and in 1972, David Johnson and **ALAN WHITTLE** were the goalscorers in a 2-1 FA Cup fourth-round victory.

As well as Vinny Samways, other ex-Blues 'in red' include Bernie Wright, Stuart Rimmer, Mark Hughes and former reserves Danny Fox and Anthony Gerrard.

> It prepared me to understand a dressing room and to know how a dressing room full of foreign talent can be effective

within comfortable travelling distance, but the Saddlers were doing nicely when Roberto received a call that was, ultimately, to change his life.

Not many players would swap the second tier of English football for the very bottom of the entire Football League – but then Roberto Martinez did have a tendency to accept the most challenging of opportunities!

"Colin Lee approached me to say that Brian Flynn, the Swansea manager, had been on the phone and that I had the option to join them," he recalled. "I went down to meet Brian at the Ramada Jarvis Hotel and I was very impressed by him. He sold the club to me and I loved the challenge ahead."

This time the swap was the West Midlands for Glamorgan, South Wales...

COACHES MEET –
PLAN OF ACTION

(Left to right, facing Roberto) Duncan Ferguson, Richard Evans, Dennis Lawrence and Graeme Jones air their views before first-team training...

AMPLIANDO MI FORMACION DE FUTBOL

(BROADENING MY FOOTBALL EDUCATION)

The decision to move to a club two divisions below Walsall, to a side struggling for their Football League lives, proved a wise move in the long term. Roberto established himself as a Swansea City favourite, making a lasting impression on players, management and fans alike before ending his playing career a little closer to Goodison Park...

Roberto Martinez joined Swansea City at a crucial phase in the club's proud history. The Swans were struggling at the wrong end of the bottom division, and the prospect of slipping out of the Football League and into the Conference was a very real one. Brian Flynn was the manager tasked with avoiding that unthinkable scenario and he had 19 games left to secure survival.

"Brian asked me to go across and I thought it was fascinating that a manager fighting relegation from the Football League would want me to go and play for him," Roberto revealed. "I was a technical player and Brian had 19 games to keep Swansea City in the Football League. He wanted to do it playing football. That was something that I couldn't turn down.

"Many British football managers think that the only way to pull away from the threat of relegation is through

a bunch of physical players who go for a route one and percentage play. Such an approach would have been a contradiction of all I had attempted as a player and when Brian invited me to join his battle I couldn't wait."

Roberto's switch from Walsall to Swansea wasn't without its hitches though. Even after he'd arrived in the city to prepare himself for the following day's game against Lincoln City, he was withdrawn from the Swans squad after a snag in the agreement between the two clubs.

"Instead of training with my new team-mates, I had to drive back to Walsall and I had three uncertain days wondering where my football career was going next."

Thankfully, the creases in the contract were quickly ironed out and Roberto finally became a Swansea City player. Brian Flynn did turn things around with an attractive style of football but the fight for relegation still went to the very last, nerve-jangling day of the season.

"You can imagine how it was for that last game of the season," said Roberto. "I was the captain by then but we faced the scenario of the football club losing its professional status and people losing their jobs. We had played fantastic football and that final game was one of the most fantastic football experiences of my life."

The scenario was simple for Swansea. If they beat Hull City at the Vetch Field they would be safe and it would be Exeter City who went down.

"I was very, very calm," claimed Roberto. "The week before it wasn't in our own hands but we won away and other results went in our favour, so on the last day we just had to win again. We were very confident. We had been so far adrift earlier on in the season that we knew if we could take it to the final game and still have a chance to stay up then we had done well.

> **Swansea City is an incredible and passionate football club. I had gone there to enjoy the challenge of achieving our goal by playing good football. I wanted to help prove that you could do it in the lower leagues**

ROBERTO'S...
...SWANSEA CITY

Founded as Swansea Town in 1912, the Swans joined the Football League eight years later. They adopted their current monikor in 1969 to reflect Swansea's new status as a city.

The club experienced the full rollercoaster of fortunes in the late '70s-early '80s. Liverpool and Wales striker John Toshack was named manager in March 1978 at the age of 28, signalling a rapid rise of three promotions in four seasons that took the club from the Fourth to the First Division for the first time, in 1981.

Blues legend **BOB LATCHFORD** scored a hat-trick on his Swansea debut in a 5-1 victory over Leeds United, the club's first game in the top flight. They would eventually finish sixth, the highest league placing in their history. Unfortunately, by 1986, they were back in the bottom tier, coming close to going out of business.

The Swans moved to their Liberty Stadium home in 2005, having been promoted to the third tier the previous campaign. Roberto Martinez skippered the victorious Football League Trophy side in 2005/06, before taking over as manager the following season. He would lead the Swans to the League One title in 2008, consolidating their place in the second tier before leaving for Wigan Athletic in the summer of 2009.

Brendan Rodgers completed the Swans' journey back to the top flight of English football in 2011, via the play-offs. They thus became the first Welsh side to play in the Premier League.

City won their first major trophy in 2013, beating Bradford in the League Cup final.

Among the Swans' former Everton contingent are Eddie Thomas, George Kirby, Dai Davies, Neil Robinson, Gary Stanley, Warren Aspinall and Kevin McLeod.

LEE TRUNDLE: "AT FANCY-DRESS PARTIES HE WOULD BE DRESSED IN SOME INTERESTING COSTUMES..."

Lee Trundle arrived at Swansea City on a free transfer in the summer ahead of the 2003/04 campaign. He was met on his first day by the Swans' club captain, a certain Roberto Martinez.

That first day saw the pair develop a close relationship on and off the pitch, and Trundle is delighted to see his old team-mate now at the helm of his beloved Blues.

It was the Spaniard's passion that impressed Trundle, with the striker recalling a night out for dinner that helped cement their friendship.

"Rob and I got on straight away," he smiles. "We'd work together in training, then of a night we would go for a bite to eat and he would be telling me what a great club Swansea was and how I had come to the right place. He spoke like a manager, even when he was a player, and as a club captain he was someone who would certainly be listened to.

"Aside from the football, he was also a great laugh and someone who everyone liked in the dressing room. As I say, he was club captain and someone everyone looked up to as well. Although he never drank, whenever there were team-bonding days Rob would always be the first there organising the event. He was a big part of the group and a big part

looked after us off the pitch as well."

As Trundle alludes to, it was on the pitch where the pair were most in tandem. "We hit it off straight away," he recounts. "The kind of player I am, I like to get the ball into feet around the penalty area. Rob would always be looking for you with a quick pass rather than hooking the ball on, like a number of other midfielders in the division at the time. He wanted to put his foot on the ball and play football, which suited me down to the ground.

"When he got the ball he would always look to play me in. Quick free-kicks, he was very sharp in his mind and wanted to keep the ball moving in a similar way to how he manages his team. He was someone who was better than the division he was playing in at the time."

Now taking the first steps into coaching himself – at Swansea in fact – Trundle is regularly in contact with Roberto, a man who taught him so much. "Watching him as a player, observing how professional he was, he did everything like you would expect a top professional to do," he explained. "He looked after his body, he ate well, he never ate fast food – anything he did eat would be to fuel himself to play football. It is something he has carried on into coaching.

he introduced. I will certainly take a lot of what he does into my coaching as it is the way I would like my teams to play."

For now, Trundle, as a devout Blue, is delighted to be enjoying first-hand the style of football that Martinez implements at Everton, and believes he can become even better. "As an Everton fan myself, as soon as he got the job I was made up as I know how he works, know how much care he puts into the job and I know that Everton Football Club will now be his life," he concluded.

"He will help out with the community, he will get the players involved in that but most of all he will have a love for the football club.

"I think he has already showed at Everton, with the players he has been able to bring in and the style of play he has been able to implement, that he will be brilliant for us."

> He spoke like a manager, even when he was a player, and as a club captain he was someone who would certainly be listened to...Aside from football, he was also a great laugh and someone who everyone liked

of the success we had.

"We used to have our fancy-dress parties, which saw him come dressed in some interesting costumes, notably a biker-chick complete with a big fat-suit. But he was the type of guy who would muck in with the boys. Rob was also the one on those nights out who would be telling us that it was time to go home! As a club captain, he even

"I will be spending a few days at Finch Farm soon to watch how he does things because with myself going into coaching, he is someone I look up to and would like to aspire to.

"His style and thought process is exactly the way I want to play football. Rob began the system Swansea use to this day. Before that we did play football but we didn't play it like he did, with the patience

"It was a unique game where you could sense and smell the occasion. On the pitch we could feel the tension in the crowd. They probably felt that their great club was just an hour-and-a-half away from falling into the world of non-League football."

Swansea City 4 Hull City 2.

That was the final score on a very emotional afternoon. The Swans were safe!

"The final whistle was the greatest relief of my life!" said Roberto. "Survival meant so much to thousands of individuals, not just in Swansea but in many parts of the world. We played well in those last 19 games and the next aim was to try and get the club back to where it belonged – a leading club with a good philosophy.

"We had an unbelievable points return from the 19 games and that gave us the belief that we were good enough to get out of the division quite quickly."

Progress was certainly made the following season when Swansea finished 10th, but by then Kenny Jackett was the manager. Roberto was in and out of the side under Jackett.

"I don't think my style of play suited Kenny Jackett's plans. In our first league game of the season I was substituted after 55 minutes and I knew as I walked off that I wasn't going to be part of his vision for the future. From then on I faced a huge challenge. I stuck at it and battled my way back into the team, and by the end of the season I had probably played more minutes than anybody else."

Celebrating Football League Trophy success at the Millennium Stadium in 2006, and (bottom pic) in the thick of things for the Swans against Cheltenham Town

Swansea finished third to secure promotion in 2004/05 – a nice way to say farewell to the Vetch and a nice platform for life at the Liberty Stadium. Roberto captained the Swans in the very last game at the ground, a Welsh Cup final victory over Wrexham, and the very first match at the Liberty, a 1-0 win against Tranmere Rovers.

He remained unconvinced, though, that Kenny Jackett wanted him as part of his long-term strategy – and the manager actually told him as much before the start of the season. At the end of it there was no new contract on the table. It was time to move on again, but Roberto had only fond memories of the time he had spent in South Wales.

"Once you are there you realise that Swansea City is an incredible and passionate football club. There are only two professional clubs within a two-hour drive so it is very intense but a great place to enjoy your football. I had gone there to enjoy the challenge of achieving our goal by playing good football.

"People claimed that in the lower leagues you couldn't achieve anything by playing good football but I wanted to help prove that you could. All my life I had been fighting to play with my qualities that you generally wouldn't find in the lower leagues.

"Almost getting relegated was a kick in the backside for everyone at the club. The club had been very close to going into liquidation but the new owners loved it and everyone got together – players, staff, fans, everyone. The history of the club is there to see and it's a big part of the community.

"The council worked hard to get the new stadium and we had to get promotion, which we did. We won the Welsh Cup as well and then we moved into a new stadium, so that was a massive moment.

"From a personal point of view, to captain the last ever team at the Vetch and then skipper the side in the first ever game at the Liberty are great memories, especially as I was the first foreigner to captain Swansea."

The question now was, once again, where next?

"A few League One clubs expressed an interest in signing me but I decided not to join anyone in that league, as I didn't want to play against Swansea City. So I decided to sign for Chester City in League Two."

hester City Football
Club doesn't play
too big a part in the
Roberto Martinez
story but it's a club
he still has a lot of
affection for. He admits that their
subsequent demise into non-League
football saddened him.

"I could never have imagined what was
going to happen to Chester City Football
Club in the following few years," he
lamented. "At the time I was there it was
in a good position. Like every club they
had to work hard to balance the books,
but the chairman and the manager had
a very strong relationship and the club
had some stability. There was a clear
desire to try and get into the League
Two play-offs to see if we could move
higher up."

The move to Chester in the summer of
2006 saw Roberto team up with a former
manager of his.

"We had been through a very intense
period at Swansea City and I was
looking for my next football challenge.
My main reason for moving to Chester
was to be reunited with Graham Barrow,
the assistant-manager," he explained. "I
first met Graham in June 1995 in Spain

when he was the manager at Wigan
Athletic. He had flown to Barcelona and
then driven two hours to the middle of
nowhere to watch Isidro Diaz and myself
play in a cup match.

"I was very impressed with the
professionalism and determination that
he had showed. Graham had made sure
that we three Spanish boys settled in
quickly at Wigan. We were regularly
invited to his home to practise our
English with his family."

Roberto did well for the Seals, playing
31 games and collecting a few Man of
the Match awards along the way. His
plan was to see out his playing days at
Chester and then move into coaching.

"It felt like the perfect place just
to carry on enjoying my football. It
was an exciting place at that time. I
lived in Chester and I'd signed a two-
year contract when I moved back to
the North West. It was a good period
for me. I enjoyed my football and I
experimented a lot."

The most notable event during
Roberto's time at the Deva Stadium was
when Chester were beaten 3-1 by Bury
in the second round of the FA Cup but
still found themselves in the draw for
the third round! Bury had fielded an

*Above top: Deva scene:
Chester's home ground,
where Roberto ended his
playing career*

*Above: Graham Barrow
was key in Roberto's move
to Chester*

Spanish journalist Guillem Balague worked with Roberto on Sky's La Liga football coverage

ineligible player so were thrown out of the competition, with Chester re-instated. They then lost 1-0 to Ipswich Town at Portman Road in the third round.

On Wednesday 21 February 21 2007, Chester City defeated Bury 1-0 at the Deva Stadium. Roberto Martinez was named as the Man of the Match – which was entirely fitting seeing as though he never played another professional football match after that night.

Two days later he left Chester, having been offered the job of managing Swansea City.

> It felt like the perfect place just to carry on enjoying my football. It was an exciting place. I lived in Chester and it was a good period for me

LA LIGA PUNDIT

It was whilst at Chester that Roberto's punditry career really took off. He joined the Spanish football team on Sky Sports alongside regular Spanish pundit, Guillem Balague.

It had started for Roberto when the show invited him to a Spanish restaurant in London to share views on the game in Spain with Jordi Cruyff (then at Manchester United), future Chelsea defender Albert Ferrer and Balague. He enjoyed the experience and soon became a regular on the programme, watching La Liga games and then offering some post-match analysis.

"I really enjoyed it but at first I still had some worries about my broken English," said Roberto. "However, I realised the programme would put me under the right kind of pressure so I'd have to learn very quickly."

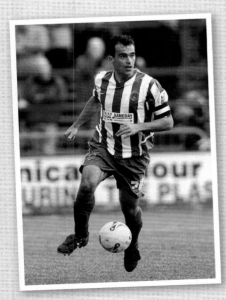

ROBERTO'S...
...CHESTER CITY

Founded in 1885, the club existed for 125 years before being disolved in March 2010. The fans reformed the current Chester FC in the wake of the club's demise two months later. They currently reside in the Conference Premier after three successive promotions.

The original club joined the Football League in 1931, competing in the bottom two divisions.

They secured their first ever promotion in 1974/75, finishing fourth in the Fourth Division, a season that also saw them reach the League Cup semi-final having beaten league champions Leeds United during their cup run.

The Seals were the first winners of the short-lived 'Debenhams Cup' in 1977, competed for by the sides from outside the top two divisions who had gone furthest during that season's FA Cup.

A youngster by the name of Ian Rush was sold to Liverpool for a club record fee in 1980. Other notable players include Arsenal and England defender, Lee Dixon.

In 1983 they adopted the 'City' monikor to reflect Chester's city status.

The club moved to the Deva Stadium in 1992. Uniquely it is based in two countries: the pitch is in Wales, while the entrance and part of the club offices are in England.

Everton's most successful skipper, KEVIN RATCLIFFE, who ended his playing career with the Seals, took over as manager in 1998 – while former Blues Mike Pejic and Ian Atkins have also managed the club.

The Conference Premier was won in 2004 – City's only league title win.

Ex-Blues at Chester have included club legend Stuart Rimmer, Michael Branch, Nick Chadwick and Tony Grant.

BOOT BOYS – GETTING READY FOR TRAINING

Leon Osman, Duncan Ferguson and Roberto don their boots ahead of first-team training...

DE ENTRAR EN LA LINEA DE FUEGO

(STEPPING INTO THE HOT SEAT)

There was little doubt in Roberto's mind that he was ready for management – and when a former club came calling he was happy to bring down the curtain on his playing career and begin a new chapter in his life...

 n 23 February 2007 Roberto Martinez became a football manager.

"I didn't even apply for the job but when I got a phone call from Swansea City I had to make the decision to give up my playing career," he said. "It was an interesting moment for me. When I got the phone call I went home and I spoke with Beth and I spoke with my family and with my best friend. My friend told me to go to bed and then see how I felt in the morning. 'See how you feel and you'll be ready to make the right decision.' That was the perfect way to face that dilemma."

The new Swansea City boss was technically a player-manager, but he quickly realised that the two jobs were far too time-consuming. Having joined Swansea City outside of the transfer window he was ineligible to play for the rest of the season. That effectively made the retirement decision for him.

"I had to fight against myself because I always used to say to anyone who would listen that a player should play for as long as he possibly can. I would tell my team-mates and my friends not to retire from playing football until you are unable to run anymore.

"I tried to kid myself and I kept my registration so I could play the following season, but deep down

AWAY
HUM YES LISTEN TO THE PEOPLE, MR PRESCOTT
61,452 PEOPLE VOTED STADIJM YES LIST N TO THE PE PRESCOTT

Directing matters from the Swansea City dugout

I knew that I couldn't be a player-manager, I had to be a manager. I had seen player-managers in the past and I could never understand how that could work. How could a person with a high heartbeat make cool decisions during a game and assess things from a tactical point of view? It didn't happen in Spain."

Roberto was 33 years old when he played his last professional game. Gary Megson and Dean Saunders were among the other names considered for the Swansea City job but the chairman, Huw Jenkins, wanted Roberto. And Roberto wanted Swansea City.

"The only dressing room I could have gone to at that time was Swansea's because I knew them all, I knew the football club and I knew the fans," he reasoned. "I had really strong relationships and I knew I would get the patience I needed from everyone to implement my changes. I was in an advantageous situation because when a new manager meets a new dressing room you need at least six weeks to get to know all the little aspects of each player. But I knew most of them and I only had to learn about the new players who had joined after I had left.

"I felt ready because I knew exactly how I wanted to play football and I knew the things that over the years I had in my mind. I had ideas that I wanted to put into practice but it was more a case of deciding if I was ready to stop playing and become a manager. I had to accept that it would be the end of my days as a player and that it was a consequence of taking the job."

One little issue that Roberto needed to settle quite hastily was the natural familiarity that he got from the players who had been team-mates less than a year earlier.

"It was a bit difficult because they were friends who I had been sharing strong moments with as a team-mate and as a captain. It wasn't natural for them to call me gaffer so I implemented a little rule that when they called me Roberto they had to pay a £5 fine. They quickly adapted after that!

"When I met the players I knew what to expect from them. They were excited about being able to play a different way and being given the time to adapt to it."

Roberto Martinez picked a team for the very first time on Saturday 24 February 2007. Swansea were away to Yeovil Town and Dennis Lawrence, now a coach at Everton, was in that first starting XI. So were lifelong Evertonian Lee Trundle and Leon Britton, who is still in the Swans squad to this day.

Former Ipswich Town striker Marcus Stewart scored the only goal of the game to give Yeovil a victory, and Roberto admitted that he was less than impressed with what he saw.

I had ideas that I wanted to put into practice but it was more a case of deciding if I was ready to stop playing and become a manager

"I didn't like the players' body language and I didn't like their lack of enjoyment at being on the pitch," he said. "Having played with most of the players the previous season I knew what they were capable of doing. I realised that I had to bring them back to a place where they could once again enjoy their football, but also be very competitive."

Three days later, Swansea beat Rotherham United 2-1 away from home. Roberto Martinez and Swansea City were up and running!

"It was an interesting period. We had 12 games to try and get into the play-offs and it went down to the last match of the season. We got an incredible response from the players and we only missed out in the end by three points. Looking back, those 12 games were perfect to prepare us for the next season. They gave me the ideal opportunity to see what was needed. I was able to sign 10 players that summer and that set the foundations for the Swansea City that would play their football."

After the loss to the Glovers, Roberto guided Swansea to seven wins and three draws from their next 11 matches to give themselves an outside chance of making the play-offs on the last day of the season.

"Although we came close it was probably a good thing that we just missed out on the play-offs because we weren't yet ready for the step-up. The final game was an exciting one though!"

To describe Swansea's last fixture of the 2006/07 campaign as 'exciting' is probably an understatement! The Swans put three goals past a young goalkeeper on loan from Manchester City called Joe Hart – but the visitors, Blackpool, bagged six goals of their own!

"I gave a professional debut to a young man called Joe Allen that day too," smiled Roberto.

CHAMPION & INNOVATOR

During the summer of 2007, Roberto Martinez brought in 10 new players and allowed several to leave the Liberty Stadium. Angel Rangel, Warren Feeney and Jason Scotland were among the new faces, but the opener at Oldham Athletic ended in a 2-1 defeat. Things got better from then on though and Swansea stormed to the League One title, finishing 10 points clear of second-placed Nottingham Forest.

In October 2007 he won his first Manager of the Month award, he retained it for November and, unsurprisingly, he was named as the League One Manager of the Year. It all seemed to come very easily for him!

"No, no, no...never," he smiled. "You need to understand that the margins are so small and that we were very fortunate to be really successful and break records at a club that had glorious years in the past. You could see that we were getting stronger and getting better and the rewards were welcome. But it was just part of keeping focus on getting the football club into the Premier League.

"Other clubs had bigger budgets. Leeds United and Nottingham Forest were our rivals. Leeds had been punished by 15 points and they had appealed so my target for my team was to finish at least 16 points ahead of Leeds in case they won their appeal and got the points back. We did that, we finished exactly 16 points ahead of them."

Swansea clinched promotion with four games to spare but it was tinged with a little bit of regret when they actually clinched the title a few days later despite losing 2-1 at home to Yeovil.

"It was a bit of a let-down," Roberto admitted. "You always learn in football that you learn things the hard way. We wanted to beat Yeovil at home to secure promotion but we lost.

In discussion with England boss Roy Hodgson, then manager of Fulham

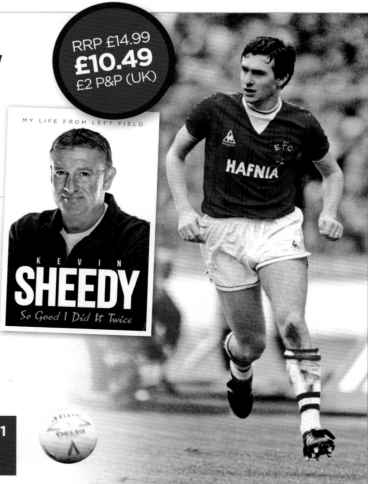

Every season presented me with a new challenge... People said that a newly-promoted side like Swansea could never survive unless they spent money

"But because results went our way we got promoted anyway, but it was a bit of an anti-climax. The players celebrated promotion but they were also disappointed that we hadn't managed to win the game.

"I knew then that the group of players were ready to achieve something special. We'd lost a very tight game and the players didn't feel quite right celebrating promotion. They had magnificent character."

The success was rewarded with an open-topped bus parade through the streets of Swansea. "It was the same bus that was used in 1981 to celebrate John Toshack's team reaching the top division for the first time in the Swans' history," said Roberto.

But it hadn't all been plain sailing for Swansea. They needed to beat Havant & Waterlooville in an FA Cup replay to secure a visit to Anfield in the next round– but the non-Leaguers won 4-2. But that was no more than a blip. The Swans were very much heading in the right direction.

Lifting the League One trophy in 2008

"Every season presented me with a new challenge," said Roberto. "The first season was how we could change the football philosophy without having much money. Then we wanted to bring in foreign talent to compliment the British core of the team. We did that really well. We got Dutch players and Spanish players but we always kept a British core.

"Then when we got promotion, people on the outside said we couldn't play our style in the Championship and that we had to bring in more new players. They said that a newly-promoted side like Swansea could never survive unless they spent money.

"My focus was to play the way we had in League One with the same players, with one or two additions. We finished just outside the play-offs in our first season, playing some great football. The DNA of that group was really strong."

Football clubs were beginning to sit up and take notice of Roberto Martinez, and his name was regularly linked with managerial vacancies.

"Yes, it was. There were rumours in the press but in the summer of 2009 it was Celtic who agreed compensation with Swansea at the same time as Wigan Athletic. I met Celtic first and then I met Dave Whelan. There were another two clubs, too, West Brom and Birmingham City.

"As a manager you know when it's the right time to go. You also know when it's the right time for your football club. Sometimes managers are always ready to jump to the next challenge for themselves but I wasn't like that. Any move had to be right for both parties – for me and the football club. It was the right time at Swansea. The money they received for me allowed them to move on again."

The Celtic link was obviously as tempting as it must have been flattering for Roberto but once he met up with Dave Whelan, the man who brought him to England, there was only one destination for him – and it wasn't going to be Glasgow.

"The way Dave Whelan is, he just rang me and told me that he wanted me to come and manage his team," Roberto revealed. "We hadn't been in contact with each other for a while but then when we met it was as if we had spoken the day before! It is a strong bond and I always felt a strong loyalty to him because he brought me to the British game. It wasn't a hard decision to make."

CLOSE TO THE ACTION - TRAINING

Roberto keeps tabs on his notes as the first team's training session gets underway at Finch Farm

VOLVER DONDE EMPEZO TODO

(BACK WHERE IT ALL BEGAN)

I n August 2009, Roberto Martinez took his seat at English football's top table. He was a Premier League manager and he got off to a flyer with a 2-0 win away to Aston Villa in his first game in charge of Wigan Athletic.

The remit for Wigan Athletic during their top-flight tenure was to remain in the Premier League. They managed it in Roberto's first season and enjoyed some great occasions along the way, with wins against Chelsea, Liverpool and Arsenal.

"When I arrived at Wigan, the first thing I had done was to look through the recent history and see what the team had achieved," said Roberto.

"The first thing that shocked me was that at that time Wigan had never beaten one of the so-called top four in the Premier League in 33 attempts. I knew that it must be a mental block and we had to work on that. That was a great challenge and to beat those sides we had to be tactically and technically perfect, and we had to be perfect mentally as well. I was really delighted when we beat Chelsea. It was the first time that Carlo Ancelotti had been beaten at Chelsea. Then we were able to defeat Liverpool for the first time.

"Remember, I had been there as a player. We had that conversation many times when fans would tell me how they had watched the team in their non-League days. That was all fresh in my mind when I went back as a manager and everything we achieved with Wigan, we did it by breaking new ground. Beating top four teams at home, beating them away, staying in the Premier League season after season was all brand new. That's what football is all about – creating memories for the fans and creating teams that the fans can be truly proud of.

"Those four years at Wigan were

phenomenal. We had to be perfect at times in every aspect of our performances to win some of the games. I was very fortunate with the support I had from Dave Whelan because he knew we had to get through some tough periods to reach those highs."

At the end of the 2010/11 season, Wigan needed two wins from their last two games to negotiate their way out of relegation trouble. They duly got them.

"Football can go down to very small margins," said Roberto. "We had to play West Ham at home and Stoke City away. West Ham were fighting to stay up and Stoke had the opportunity to finish in the top 10 of the Premier League for the first time in their history. Nobody had won at the Britannia that calendar year. We were 2-0 down at half-time against West Ham and we were relegated at that time. We came back to win 3-2, and then we went to Stoke and won 1-0."

The 2011/12 had a particularly spectacular climax to it for the Wigan faithful. With nine games to go, the Latics were adrift at the foot of the table. Among those remaining nine fixtures were visits to Anfield

> **Everything we achieved with Wigan, we did it by breaking new ground. Beating top four teams at home, beating them away, staying in the Premier League season after season was all brand new for the fans**

JASON KOUMAS: "ROBERTO MADE YOU FEEL LIKE A MILLION DOLLARS GOING INTO A GAME..."

When Steve Bruce decided to leave Wigan Athletic for Sunderland, Jason Koumas and the rest of the Latics squad waited for the news concerning who would replace him. The decision had to be right, for Bruce had arguably over-achieved at the DW Stadium.

So when the name 'Roberto Martinez' was brought up, Welsh international Koumas did his research on the then Swansea City manager.

> He is so positive and that rubs off on everyone. He won't let his head go down or the players' heads go down

"I knew a couple of the lads who he had managed at Swansea," he recalls. "I think everyone knew by the time he was coming into the club that he was a football man and that suited my game. It was music to my ears when I found out he was taking over.

"I remember him coming in. He had a talk with the lads, one-on-one, which is how Roberto tends to go about things. He wanted to know a lot about each player as a person.

"He had big shoes to fill, but he filled them very well. From day one you could see how impressed the lads were with his training methods and how he wanted to play. His man-management was different to Steve Bruce's – he did a lot of one-on-one interaction, talked to you about your game and made you feel like a million dollars going into a game. I believe that to be his biggest asset.

"But the way he wants to play the game is what is making him so well thought of as a manager."

So Evertonians are finding out. The style of football employed by the Spaniard has won over the terraces, but he already had a fan in Koumas.

"No matter who we were playing, there was a certain method of play that he wanted," he added. "That is his football philosophy, playing attacking football. I remember a game against Arsenal at the Emirates towards the end of that season and Wigan were different class. They passed Arsenal to death, which was something he drilled into us as soon as he arrived at the club.

"It is a funny thing – we did take a few heavy defeats but he always approached the next game as though you had won the previous one 5-0. He is so positive and I think that rubs off on everyone. He won't let his head go down or the players' heads go down, he still goes about things the same way."

Koumas admits Martinez is a man he can still turn to for advice, should he need it, such is his high opinion of his former manager. He is also unsurprised at the impact the former Latics midfielder has had at Everton.

"He did a great job at Wigan," he concludes. "Yes, they got relegated but the job he did there was unbelievable.

"What he is now doing at Everton, the way he is changing the style of play so quickly, is of no surprise to me because I have seen it first-hand every day."

The respect the Everton fans showed Wigan and the way they clapped the players off was incredible. There was a lot of hurt because Everton had huge expectations but I felt that it was a club that I wanted to be involved with

and the Emirates, as well as a home game with Manchester United. Astonishingly, Wigan won all three of those games and picked up a total of 20 points from the nine matches.

"I enjoyed those moments," said Roberto. "We decided to make a mini-league when we had nine games left, including Liverpool, Manchester United, Arsenal, Chelsea and Newcastle United. We knew that physically we were okay and the mentality was terrific. We finished top of that nine-game league with seven wins and two defeats, which is incredible. That gave me the understanding that in football you don't rely on finances. Wigan was the proof. We worked hard and the players fully understood how we wanted to perform in every game. We

were tactically very aware and we had thinkers on the pitch. It was outstanding for us."

The finest hour was, of course, yet to come. Wigan Athletic became a Football League club in 1978 after winning the Northern Premier League. In 2013, they won the FA Cup.

On 11 May 2013 Wigan Athletic travelled to Wembley for an FA Cup final showdown with Manchester City. The Latics were high-priced underdogs but in the battle of the Roberto's, it was Martinez who out-thought and defeated Mancini. Ben Watson's 90th-minute header won the trophy for Wigan.

"We were playing an incredible side and we didn't win by luck," said Roberto. "From start to finish it was an incredible performance. Everyone wrote us off before the game, but we were following a dream. You cannot describe the feeling. At half-time we were really down because we played well and when you are playing a top team, you need to take your chances. We were feeling that maybe we had wasted our opportunity.

"Before the goal I was thinking about extra-time and how to use our man advantage. You could see the goal coming – the performance was magnificent, we deserved it. You dream of playing at Wembley and winning – the underdogs played with incredible bravery and belief and fought the odds again. That's the FA Cup."

Along the way to that amazing achievement they broke Evertonian hearts with a 3-0 demolition job at Goodison Park in the quarter-finals.

"Every time we faced Everton we were the better side but we either ended up losing or drawing the games. I always used the term 'being bullied' on the pitch by Everton.

"We prepared a lot psychologically for that FA Cup game. We had to be 'the bullies' in the first half an hour. It was a great performance but that was the day when I realised that Goodison Park was my type of place."

Wigan had dumped Everton out of the FA Cup but a little seed had been sown in the mind of Roberto Martinez.

"The respect the Everton fans showed Wigan and the way they clapped the players off the pitch was incredible. There was a lot of hurt because Everton had huge expectations of getting to Wembley but I felt that it was a football club I wanted to be involved with."

TRAINING EXERCISE – SQUAD WORK-OUT

Roberto oversees a small-sided game which includes
(left to right) Steven Pienaar, Sylvain Distin, Leon
Osman, Gareth Barry and Tony Hibbert

TOMAR EL PUESTO MAS ALTO

(TAKING ON THE TOP JOB)

Once David Moyes' departure was confirmed in May 2013, there was only one serious contender in the eyes of Everton chairman, Bill Kenwright. Roberto Martinez was his No. 1 choice to take over as new manager...

Roberto meets his new chairman

After 27 trophy-laden years as manager of Manchester United, Sir Alex Ferguson stepped down at the end of the 2012/13 season. His last act as boss at Old Trafford was to recommend David Moyes as his successor. It was an invitation that Moyes, after 11 years at Everton, couldn't turn down.

So, for the first time since appointing Moyes to succeed Walter Smith in 2002, Bill Kenwright was on the look-out for a new manager. Roberto Martinez will never forget the first time he met the Everton chairman.

"I was shocked because I thought it was impossible to find another chairman with the same love for his football club as Dave Whelan had for Wigan Athletic. I quickly realised though that Bill Kenwright had exactly the same passion for Everton. It was incredible. I wouldn't say that Everton is part of his life, Everton IS his life. That gave me such a comfort and it was perfect for me that things would work between us."

Lining up with the board members at Goodison: (Left to right) CEO Robert Elstone, Chairman Bill Kenwright, Roberto, Deputy Chairman Jon Woods, Life President Sir Philip Carter

Roberto was duly appointed as the new manager of Everton and he quickly started to understand what this magnificent football club is all about.

"It's not one thing, it has been a chain of events," he said. "The first image of walking out before the Austria Vienna friendly, for example. That was a football exercise – it wasn't even a game for me – and to see the away end full of Everton fans was incredible and something that I will never forget.

"The way that the team was supported at Accrington Stanley for a friendly was another moment. There are lots of moments that have shocked me and made me feel proud and privileged to be the manager of Everton. It drives me on even more to try and achieve something."

The supporters at Goodison Park took to their new manager straight away. 'Allez, Allez Ohhh' is regularly blasted out from the stands up and down the country wherever Everton play, and the welcome from the Evertonians is something the boss is hugely grateful for.

"I feel that it is a natural relationship. When I first read Alan Ball's quote that says: 'Once Everton has touched you

nothing is ever the same' I couldn't really understand it. But once you meet the fans here, then you understand it.

"The fans see that the way I want the game to be played belongs here at Everton. We have the School of Science and I have learned about personalities like Will Cuff, Howard Kendall and Joe Royle. I think it's a natural relationship between me and Everton and it's a perfect fit."

Meeting the fans for the first time as Everton manager outside Goodison Park

The first image I have is walking out before the Austria Vienna friendly. That was just a football exercise and to see the away end full of Everton fans was incredible and something I will never forget

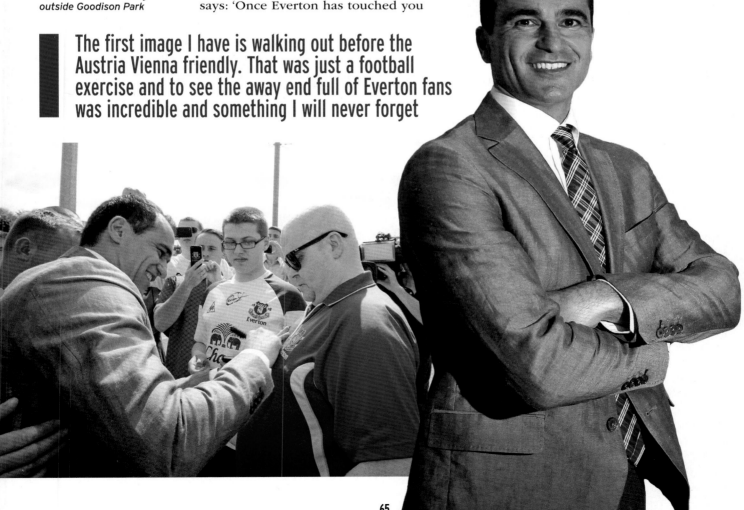

"I have already seen why David Moyes called Everton the People's Club when he came here 11 years ago"

"This is a really special day to come to Everton Football Club. The feeling already is one of excitement and honour. I want to thank the chairman and the board for giving me this opportunity. This is a phenomenal and passionate football club, and I can't wait to start"

"The chairman hasn't put any pressure on me. We have a very strong team and over the next few months we need to get together and make sure we are a winning side"

"Only 14 managers have had the honour to be at this football club. That gives you the sense of responsibility and shows you are going to get time to work; for me that is important"

"The idea of the School of Science is one of the big reasons why I feel so excited. I know about the past of Everton"

"Champions League qualification is the challenge. It just comes with the title of being Everton manager. I feel you need to have that football dream"

GRAEME JONES:
"HE HAS UNBELIEVABLE STRENGTH OF CHARACTER"

raeme Jones has worked with Roberto Martinez at three different clubs – Swansea City, Wigan Athletic and Everton. So the former goal-getting centre-forward knows his pal as well as anyone…

Why is Roberto Martinez such a good manager?

There isn't one reason, there are so many things. His love of the game is the first thing. We all love football but there's different levels of loving it and he's besotted! And his footballing education back in Spain is totally different from ours over here. If you had to define a nation, Spain would be tactical and we would be physical. He is a naturally intelligent guy and he is also very level-headed. He thinks 'outside the box' and is really creative. He will always put his trust in you until you lose it.

Anything else?

Oh yes! He has unbelievable strength of character that people don't see very often. His will-to-win is incredible and one of the biggest things about him is that he is so stubborn! You have to have that though in his job and I see it as a strength and not a weakness because it makes him so single minded.

A manager and his assistant presumably fall out from time to time! It must happen to you and Roberto?

When we first started together it was every week! We were young

Graeme (below and bottom picture) with Roberto in contrasting mood on the sidelines...

68

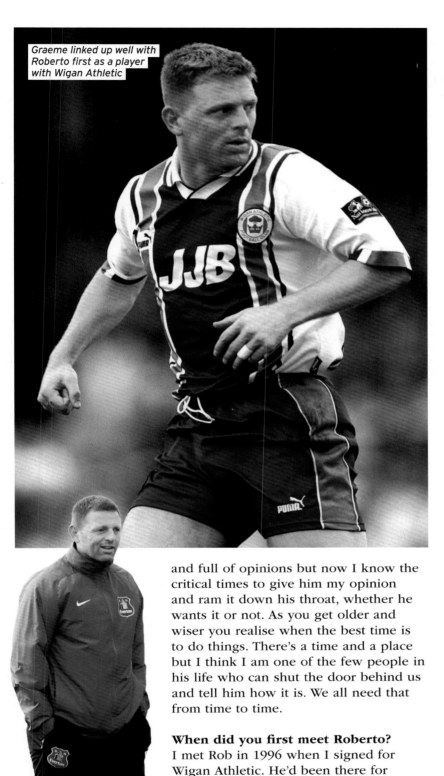

Graeme linked up well with Roberto first as a player with Wigan Athletic

pace and strength. If I made a run, Rob would put the ball on the end of my toe. We had a bond together immediately, even though we had different backgrounds and were different people. We became really good friends. We won the Third Division and stayed together for three years.

Didn't you have a relegation battle when you were both playing in Scotland?
Yes, we did when he was at Motherwell and I was playing for St Johnstone. I had been out injured for a long time and came back for the last few months of the season. I played against him at Motherwell and we lost 2-0, which was a killer for us. It was strange being on the same pitch as him as an enemy!

As you became firm friends, was the plan always to team up in management?
I had always said to Rob that when I became a manager I would take him with me as my assistant! It was strange when it happened the other way round because Rob is four years younger than me. But he was always someone who I would listen to for advice. He'd met me a week before he got the Swansea job to tell me he had a chance and to keep myself ready. To be fair though, I was in no rush to move at the time. I was the assistant-manager at Hamilton Academical and we had a good young team that included James McCarthy. I was enjoying it but I decided to join him and we've been together since.

So it was an easy decision to come here to Everton with him?
I had other offers but my relationship is with Rob and I am loyal to that. I've had a few offers over the last seven years but my conscience always gets the better of me and I am committed to my relationship with him. To come to a club like this was great...and we were ready for it.

When you're away from football situations, what does Roberto like to talk about?
Football! Watching football on the television or talking about it. That's how he lives his life. And he has got a really good sense of humour that people don't always see. He's the same person at home as he is in work.

and full of opinions but now I know the critical times to give him my opinion and ram it down his throat, whether he wants it or not. As you get older and wiser you realise when the best time is to do things. There's a time and a place but I think I am one of the few people in his life who can shut the door behind us and tell him how it is. We all need that from time to time.

When did you first meet Roberto?
I met Rob in 1996 when I signed for Wigan Athletic. He'd been there for a year when I joined from Doncaster Rovers. I remember during pre-season when the manager told us to pick a partner for some stretching me and Rob picked each other. We hit it off from that moment.

Did you enjoy playing in the same team as him?
Yes, I did. On the pitch we had great chemistry. He had a great forward pass and I had a bit of

JOE ROYLE:
"ROBERTO WAS ALWAYS NO. 1 ON BILL'S LIST..."

oe Royle knows exactly what it is to feel the excitement of preparing to take over the manager's hot seat at Everton Football Club. The only difference between Royle and Roberto Martinez is the former Blues striker was already part of the fabric at Goodison Park.

However, the trepidation, the exhilaration and the honour of taking over as manager remains the same, and Royle has been impressed with how the Spaniard has handled his move from Wigan.

But what would Martinez have been feeling in the days leading up to his appointment as David Moyes' replacement?

"I think initially he would have felt a little bit of sadness that he was leaving Wigan," admits Royle. "He had had a great time there and a great relationship with Dave Whelan. When you have a chairman that you work with and you trust, it's a

big wrench to leave that, believe me.

"But equally, Roberto knew that to progress – to do better in his career – he needed a bigger club with more backing and a bigger base. When Everton came along, I imagine he was delighted. It also meant that he didn't have to move from his family home in Greater Wigan.

"He would have looked at the history of the club, the terrific fan base and a far better team than he had at Wigan. Despite them beating Everton in the FA Cup last season, he would have known that man for man Everton had better players. He knew he would have a great chance of improving his own CV by matching his success, and hopefully bettering it. There were so many plus points and positives for Roberto when he spoke to Bill Kenwright. I'm close to Bill and, from what I can gather, Roberto was always number one on his list."

Since Roberto's Goodison unveiling, Royle has been very impressed at the way the manager has handled himself.

"He has been very calm and collected,

(Top) Joe at his desk during his tenure as Everton manager, from 1994-1997

and I love his touchline manner," said the 1995 FA Cup-winning boss. "We have seen that not all managers can behave themselves. I know through a friend of mine, who is an assessor of referees, that Roberto is very popular among match officials. There is never any direct criticism of them from him, never any ranting and raving, any prompting of the fourth official. So all round he is a very nice guy. He has come in with a smile and made more smiles."

Roberto has done that through the players, who overcame an opening run of three draws to kick-start their season with a win over Chelsea at Goodison. Royle has, like the rest of us, enjoyed the ride ever since. "He has very quickly been able to change the style of the side," he enthused. "We were never route one with David Moyes but it was a little bit more safety orientated in so much as we got the ball forward an awful lot more.

"When we went on tour in pre-season, it was obvious that Everton were trying out this new system whereby the back four spread, look for the ball and try and play passing football. There was bound to be occasions where you fall foul. But what impressed me an awful lot was when we did lose a goal because we were playing this way – e.g. against

Sunderland when Ossie was caught on the edge of the box, which probably cost us the game and there were no comebacks, no recriminations. It was just: 'Keep on with it, keep passing it'. Roberto has his principles, he knows what he wants and it's working a treat.

"He wouldn't have been worried with those early results because you have got to look at the bigger picture. You will be hurt by individual results but equally, if you know what you want then you have got to go forward and look beyond one, two or even three results. He came in with split views – some people said 'fantastic' because he had won the FA Cup, others pointed to the fact he had been relegated.

"That win against Chelsea did settle the nerves a little bit. I didn't manage to see that one and I am told that we had played better in other games and only drawn. But having that big 'W' next to your name, the sooner that one comes the better. Beating Chelsea and also losing to them in February, having lost nothing in defeat, just shows the progress. Chelsea, I would say, are just marginal favourites for the title and there is nothing between us and them. So quite honestly the win over Chelsea was a massive statement."

Given that Royle is the last Everton manager to win silverware, it was only right to ask him whether Roberto Martinez can take over that mantle. "A lot depends on finances available," he admits. "He is working with a great chairman who will support him to the hilt, and I mean that.

"To get to that next level, we probably need a 20-goal striker. The midfield players are good, defensively we are solid and there are young players coming through. Everything is going well so far and the club is going forward. The fans are loving what they are seeing, with the exciting players that are coming in. Roberto had a great window when he signed Lukaku, James McCarthy and my Player of the Year so far, Gareth Barry. So that endeared him to the fans – but the only thing now is that he has set very high standards and everyone will be wondering who he brings in next!

"So going forward immediately, I am very proud to be the last Everton manager to win a trophy but, quite honestly, I am fed up with the record, which will be 20 years next year. So let's go and do that Roberto!"

MEETING UP WITH AN EVERTON LEGEND

Roberto meets the Blues' most successful manager,
Howard Kendall, a man who he hopes to emulate by
bringing silverware back to Goodison

DENNIS LAWRENCE:
"HE WAS VERY DETAILED IN EVERYTHING HE DID..."

ennis Lawrence has a few 'firsts' behind him. He played in Trinidad & Tobago's first ever World Cup game in 2006, he played for Wrexham on the night Wayne Rooney scored his first goals as a professional footballer and he played in the first team that Roberto Martinez selected as a manager. Dennis and Roberto go back a long way.

"I first met the gaffer when I played against him. He was at Swansea and I was playing for Wrexham. I then met him properly when he took over from Kenny Jackett as manager of Swansea. My first impression was that he was very detailed in everything he did. He spoke very well, too. He knew all about my background, which was very pleasing for me."

When Roberto returned to the Liberty Stadium as the manager he was in control

of friends he had played alongside less than a year earlier.

"That must have been strange for him," said Dennis. "I wasn't one of the players who had played with him but there was a lot of optimism and excitement among those who had."

Dennis is a first-team coach at Everton now and it was Roberto who gave him his first break in that side of things.

"I only got interested in coaching when I left Swansea," said Dennis. "I played for two seasons at Swansea and then went to Crewe on loan. I hadn't been playing regularly and I told Roberto that I wanted to go out on loan, which he fully understood. While I was at Crewe I realised that I didn't have the same drive or desire to be a player but I still wanted to affect the games in a different way.

"My contract at Swansea was up and when I finished at Crewe I went home on vacation and ended up playing for a

Dennis watches on alongside head of performance, Richard Evans and assistant-boss, Graeme Jones

Once the opportunity arose to come to Everton with the gaffer it was never a question of whether I was going to come or not

local team in Trinidad. I played for three months and during that time I realised 100% that coaching was the next step.

"In 2010 I went on my B licence course with the Welsh FA at Cardiff and Roberto was a guest speaker. We had a good chat and he reminded me that he'd told me at Swansea that if I ever wanted to go into coaching there would be a place for me on his staff. On that course he told me to start to prepare myself because a call would be coming soon. Sure enough he contacted me and asked me to join him at Wigan.

"I have always been a professional person and so has the gaffer and we've always had a really good understanding. I knew what he wanted and he knew my capabilities and what I could do for him."

Dennis had his work cut out when he teamed up with Roberto at Wigan but he thoroughly enjoyed the learning curve that the manager had carefully laid out for him.

"It was a tough development process for me because I was working with the Under-21s and the first team at Wigan," Dennis explained. "There were a lot of

sessions and it was very demanding but it was the best thing that happened to me."

What also helped is that the Martinez style of football sat very comfortably with Dennis.

"The funny thing is that my background of playing football in Trinidad, we played that way. We played good football and it was difficult for me to learn the 'British' game when I first came over and played for Wrexham. So it was easy for me to coach with Roberto because I had been used to the style he likes from an early age."

When Roberto got the Goodison call, Dennis admitted that it was a very easy decision to make when he was invited to join Everton himself.

"Without a shadow of a doubt," he confirmed. "From the moment the opportunity arose to come to Everton with the gaffer it was never a question of whether I was going to come or not."

But does a football-mad person like Roberto Martinez ever switch off?

"Yes he does, when we have off-time or down-time," Dennis grinned. "He is a very professional man and that's got him to where he is now. He's one of the top managers not just in Britain but the world. He's just a normal guy when we go out for a meal or have a family get-together. He likes a laugh, he's very down-to-earth."

CLIVE TYLDESLEY: "HE PASSED WITH FLYING COLOURS..."

Clive Tyldesley covered the Merseyside patch for Radio City in the 1980s when our area really was the capital of the football world. He has been ITV's leading commentator since 1998 and knows a good manager when he sees one. He hasn't been surprised at how well Roberto Martinez has done at Goodison Park.

"I am not at all surprised at how well he's done for two reasons," he said. "Firstly he's a very thorough and thoughtful manager. He will have been considering the challenge of a step-up from Wigan Athletic for a year or two. He would have been asking himself what he needed to do to move on to the responsibilities and expectations that come with managing a club like Everton.

"Secondly, Everton were in good shape when he took over. He didn't

take over a club that was struggling to stay in the Premier League, he went to a club that was on the verge of challenging for honours. David had been in charge for so long and I think the club was probably open to a slight change of direction and emphasis."

Clive commentated on Roberto's finest hour when he sat in the Wembley gantry and watched as Wigan Athletic defeated Manchester City in the FA Cup final in 2013. He was very impressed at the way the underdogs beat the billionaires.

"I thought that his performance in that final really moved him up a notch," claimed Clive. "He speaks well and that's why ITV like to use him (!). But to make a couple of tactical changes on the day, to basically outthink Manchester City with a team

built from a fraction of the resources and to deservedly win it was terrific. He passed that challenge with flying colours.

"People say that he is a brave manager but I call it a conviction rather than bravery. He believes that having given every thought and every attention to detail, then he'll probably be right with his final conclusion as he prepares for a game. That certainty and clearness of thought is what makes him so good."

10 EVERTON MOMENTS

We've selected some memorable shots from an eventful first season under Roberto Martinez, and included what the manager said in the wake of key victories and occasions...

01

"It was a special game, a special opposition and a very good performance. We gave away two or three chances from not keeping the ball well enough but the way we reacted, took responsibility - and defensively we were immense. Throughout the game we always carried a threat and I thought we were unfortunate not to score more than one goal"

"Collecting three points here is something we haven't done for a long time so it gives you a little bit of extra feeling that I want the fans to share. There is a real sense of pride"

02

03

"It's important we have closed the window and are stronger than what we were when it started. When you have got top performers and players there is going to be interest. The window is over and there is a good opportunity to concentrate on football"

04

"West Ham wanted to stop us playing and we had to find a way to change that. We were refreshed in the second half, had more composure and looked more threatening. It didn't surprise me because you get rewards when you work really hard and we did that"

"We needed to get on the ball and we were finding it very difficult. **Leon Osman opened that up and gave us the opportunity to control the game. Leon is someone with incredible technical ability that he can use those spaces really well**"

05

"**I always measure the side by how they react to adversity and if they keep doing the right things when things don't go your way.** It would have been easy to feel sorry for ourselves, panic and lose. We were more focused than ever"

06

07

"In the second half we had more intent on the ball. I don't underestimate the size of this result. It is a magnificent three points, down to the character, resilience and belief that the players had. You look at the quality of Ross Barkley and the way Seamus Coleman has a massive impact in the final third. It's very pleasing"

08

"Kevin found it frustrating because he was surrounded by Aston Villa players. You could see the way they were set up they were trying to stop him and us really high up the pitch. Kevin worked hard without getting any joy but the way he took that free-kick showed he is a player who is ready to control moments when you can win. It shows you his character"

09

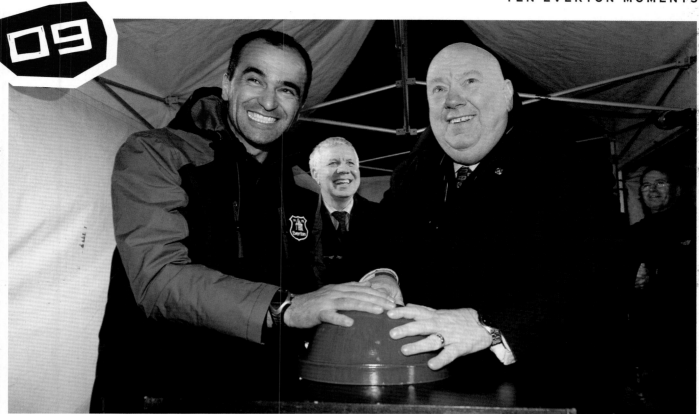

"Our fans will tell you the tower is a special sign and where everything started – not just for Everton, but for football in the city. It's a good moment for what we are about at Everton – the community and tradition, the history of our Club"

10

"We wanted to surprise Annie but she surprised me with her knowledge and passion. She is 93 and a true Evertonian. It's a privilege to be manager and I want to know what the fans think and what they want from the club. The quicker I get to know what they want – and to take advantage of the history and the fans' passion – then that will be for the better"

ONCE EVERTON HAS TOUCHED YOU...

Thanks for reading – and here's to creating more wonderful moments with you, the supporters.

Sólo lo mejor

Roberto Martinez